SHE COULDN'T
BE
GOOD!

PETER PAUPER PRESS, INC.
WHITE PLAINS, NEW YORK

Designed by Heather Zschock

Cover and page1 illustration:
Pulp Image copyright © 1995-1999 Jeffrey Luther/PC Design.
www.pulpcards.com. All rights reserved.
Publisher's name and logo are trademarks
of their respective holder.

Copyright © 2005
Peter Pauper Press, Inc.
202 Mamaroneck Avenue
White Plains, NY 10601
All rights reserved
ISBN 1-59359-396-1
Printed in China
7 6 5 4

Visit us at www.peterpauper.com

SHE JUST COULDN'T
HELP IT

YOU COULDN'T BE
MORE WRONG ABOUT ME

I'M NOT SUPPOSED TO TALK
TO YOU, YOU KNOW

SHE ALWAYS GOT WHAT SHE WANTED, AND SHE ALWAYS WANTED WHAT WASN'T HERS

OF COURSE YOU
CAN TRUST ME

LET THEM TALK

SHE WAS ALWAYS WILLING TO
GIVE A LITTLE, TO GET A LOT

SHE WAS SWEET, DISCREET, AND
NOT AT ALL WHAT YOU EXPECTED

SHE WAS AVAILABLE
FOR THE ASKING

I HAVE SO MUCH TO TELL THAT I DON'T KNOW WHERE TO BEGIN

SHE JUST COULDN'T HELP IT

YOU COULDN'T BE
MORE WRONG ABOUT ME

I'M NOT SUPPOSED TO TALK TO YOU, YOU KNOW

SHE ALWAYS GOT WHAT SHE WANTED,
AND SHE ALWAYS WANTED WHAT WASN'T HERS

LET THEM TALK

SHE WAS ALWAYS WILLING TO
GIVE A LITTLE, TO GET A LOT

SHE WAS SWEET, DISCREET, AND
NOT AT ALL WHAT YOU EXPECTED

SHE WAS AVAILABLE
FOR THE ASKING

I HAVE SO MUCH TO TELL
THAT I DON'T KNOW WHERE TO BEGIN

SHE JUST COULDN'T
HELP IT

YOU COULDN'T BE
MORE WRONG ABOUT ME

I'M NOT SUPPOSED TO TALK
TO YOU, YOU KNOW

SHE ALWAYS GOT WHAT SHE WANTED, AND SHE ALWAYS WANTED WHAT WASN'T HERS